WDS

W9-AUY-522

STAGE 2

# Who Lives

# in an Alligator Hole?

by Anne Rockwell • illustrated by Lizzy Rockwell

Collins
*An Imprint of* HarperCollins*Publishers*

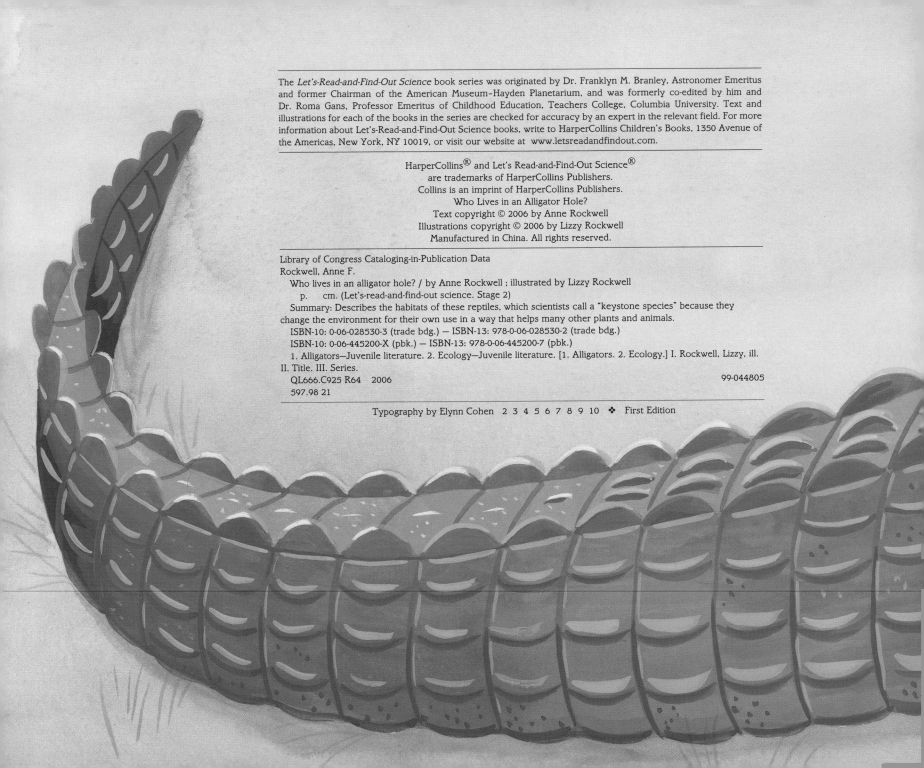

The *Let's-Read-and-Find-Out Science* book series was originated by Dr. Franklyn M. Branley, Astronomer Emeritus and former Chairman of the American Museum–Hayden Planetarium, and was formerly co-edited by him and Dr. Roma Gans, Professor Emeritus of Childhood Education, Teachers College, Columbia University. Text and illustrations for each of the books in the series are checked for accuracy by an expert in the relevant field. For more information about Let's-Read-and-Find-Out Science books, write to HarperCollins Children's Books, 1350 Avenue of the Americas, New York, NY 10019, or visit our website at www.letsreadandfindout.com.

HarperCollins® and Let's Read-and-Find-Out Science®
are trademarks of HarperCollins Publishers.
Collins is an imprint of HarperCollins Publishers.
Who Lives in an Alligator Hole?
Text copyright © 2006 by Anne Rockwell
Illustrations copyright © 2006 by Lizzy Rockwell
Manufactured in China. All rights reserved.

Library of Congress Cataloging-in-Publication Data
Rockwell, Anne F.
    Who lives in an alligator hole? / by Anne Rockwell ; illustrated by Lizzy Rockwell
        p.      cm. (Let's-read-and-find-out science. Stage 2)
    Summary: Describes the habitats of these reptiles, which scientists call a "keystone species" because they change the environment for their own use in a way that helps many other plants and animals.
    ISBN-10: 0-06-028530-3 (trade bdg.) — ISBN-13: 978-0-06-028530-2 (trade bdg.)
    ISBN-10: 0-06-445200-X (pbk.) — ISBN-13: 978-0-06-445200-7 (pbk.)
    1. Alligators—Juvenile literature. 2. Ecology—Juvenile literature. [1. Alligators. 2. Ecology.] I. Rockwell, Lizzy, ill.
II. Title. III. Series.
    QL666.C925 R64    2006                                                                                      99-044805
    597.98 21

Typography by Elynn Cohen   2  3  4  5  6  7  8  9  10   ❖   First Edition

For Dave, John, and Jimmy Jensen of Captiva Island

Special thanks to the park rangers at Everglades National Park,
in particular Maureen McGee-Ballinger and Frankie
Aranzamendi for their invaluable advice
and assistance.

—A.R. and L.R.

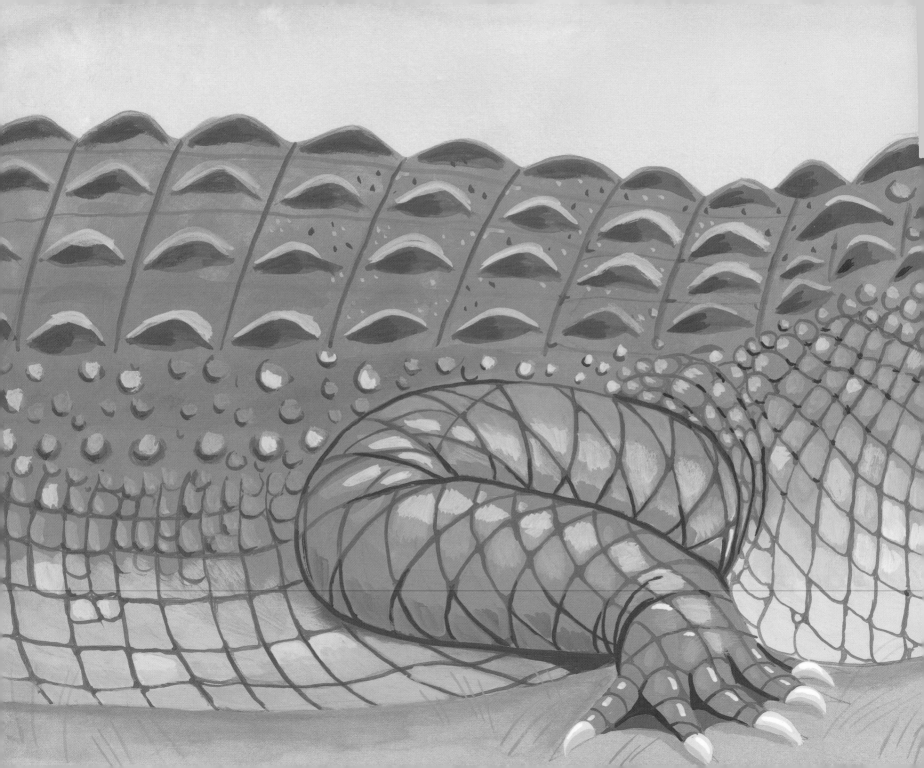

What do you know about alligators? That they are scary looking, with big jaws and sharp teeth? What do you think they're good for? Gator wrestling? Being made into shoes, purses, and wallets? Being fried for supper?

Alligators are good for more than that.

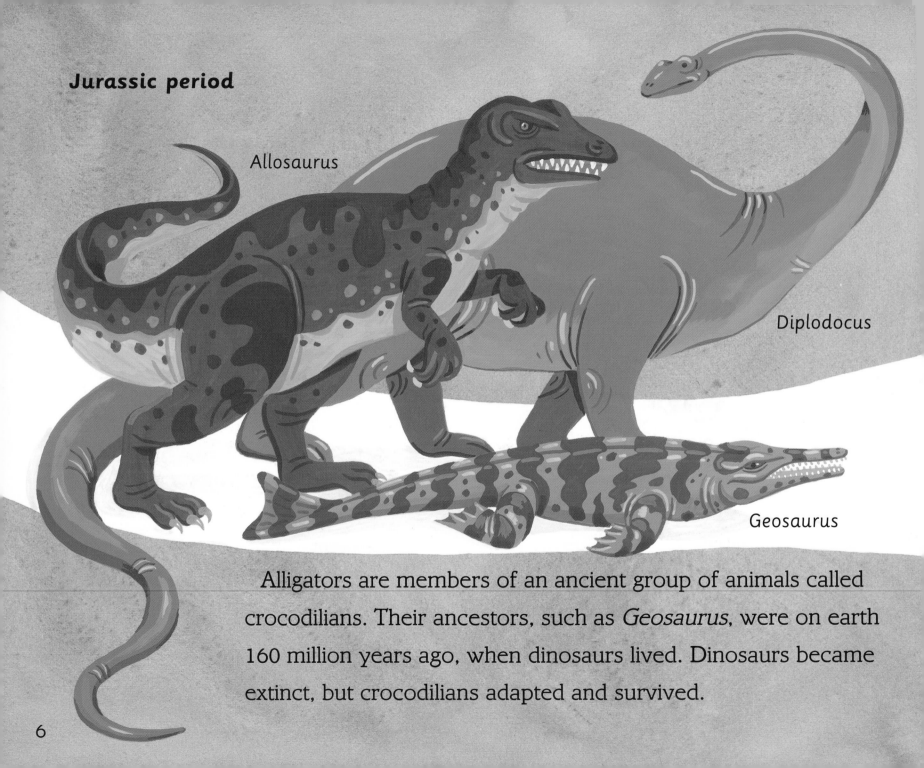

**Jurassic period**

Allosaurus

Diplodocus

Geosaurus

Alligators are members of an ancient group of animals called crocodilians. Their ancestors, such as *Geosaurus*, were on earth 160 million years ago, when dinosaurs lived. Dinosaurs became extinct, but crocodilians adapted and survived.

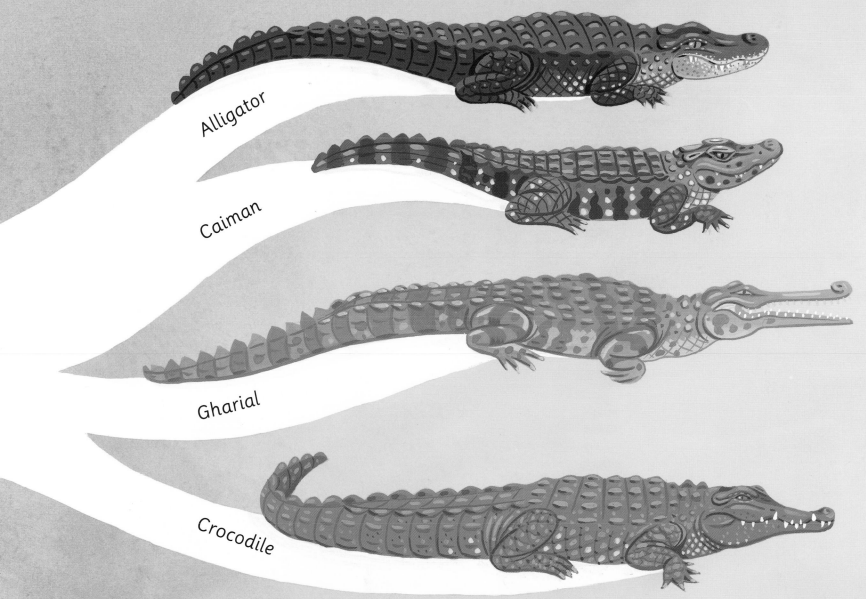

Alligator

Caiman

Gharial

Crocodile

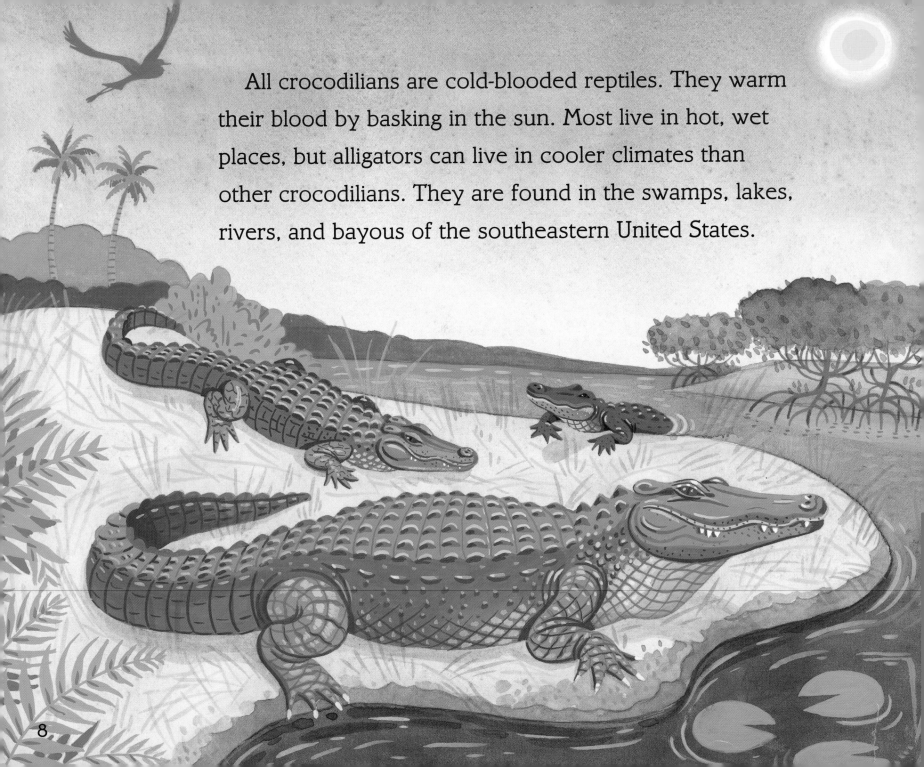

All crocodilians are cold-blooded reptiles. They warm their blood by basking in the sun. Most live in hot, wet places, but alligators can live in cooler climates than other crocodilians. They are found in the swamps, lakes, rivers, and bayous of the southeastern United States.

For a long time people thought American alligators were the only kind in the world. Then about one hundred years ago, alligators were discovered in China. Chinese alligators are shorter and fatter than American ones.

More alligators live in Florida than anywhere else. In the Everglades there is a wet season, when it rains every day. There is also a dry season, when it hardly rains at all. The ground is covered with saw grass and muck. Underneath the muck is mud. Underneath the mud is limestone. Underneath the limestone is fresh water. In some places there is a hollow in the limestone a few feet deep, where underground water can seep up through the stone.

Porous limestone bedrock

Damp muck

Wet mud

Eroded pit in limestone

Underground water can seep into gaps in limestone.

When the alligator discovers damp muck, it begins to dig. By thrashing its powerful head, tail, and body from side to side, it shoves the thick muck away.

Soon a wide hole fills with water a few feet deep. Then a lot starts to happen in the gator hole.

Fish and insects lying dormant in the wet mud wake up and lay eggs. The eggs hatch into more fish and insects. Birds come to eat them. Seeds in the bird droppings sprout. More birds and animals come to eat and drink.

When one species changes the environment for its own use in a way that helps other plants and animals, scientists call it a "keystone species." The alligator is a keystone species.

Great egret

White ibis

Anhinga

Raccoon

Purple gallinule

Great blue heron

Sunfish

Garfish

Pig frog

Minnows

Water snake

Some animals at the gator hole eat plants. Some are predators that eat other animals. The alligator is the largest. When hungry, it will eat smaller animals. But most of the time the alligator is not a danger to animals living beside it, because it doesn't eat many of them. It doesn't need to.

White ibis

Night heron

Wood stork

Little blue heron

Red-bellied turtle

Cold-blooded animals don't need to eat as often as warm-blooded ones. They don't use food to keep their blood warm the way birds and mammals do.

In winter alligators eat only about once a month. If the air temperature drops below 52 degrees Fahrenheit, they can't digest food. On cold and cloudy days they sleep in the dens they dig near the water's edge and keep warm.

The alligator eats animals that live near it, but not enough
to harm the population. In fact the alligator helps balance
everything. It eats raccoons that would have eaten too many
birds' eggs. It eats large fishes that would have eaten many
small ones.

VINTAGE FASHIONS

CIRCA 1925

By the time people understood how important alligators were
to the environment, there weren't many left. Their skins had
been fashionable all over the world for about a hundred years.
Millions had been killed. More and more were being hunted
each night.

24

People also thought the wetlands where alligators live weren't good for much, so they decided to get rid of them.

Engineers built canals and made dams, until much of the wild southern wetlands were turned into farms, roads, malls, houses, and golf courses. By the 1960s alligators were on their way to extinction.

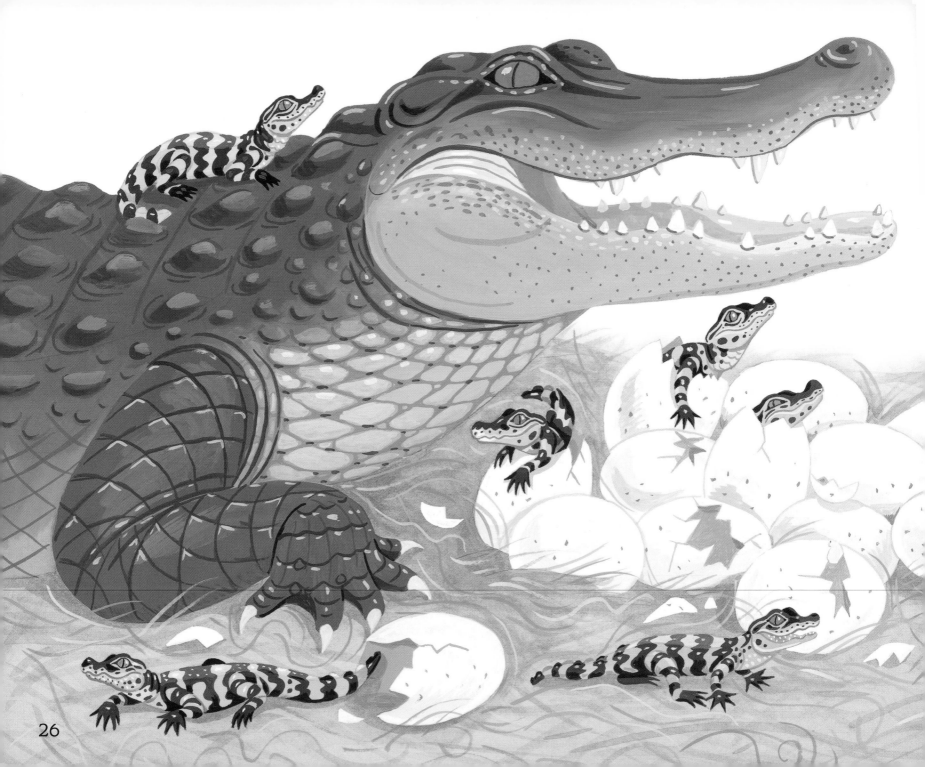

When a keystone species disappears, other species that depend on it may also disappear. Laws were passed to protect alligators. It became illegal to hunt them, or buy and sell their skins in the United States. But poachers still hunted them illegally, because people in other countries paid good money for the skins.

Finally, many other countries agreed not to buy alligator skins, or any products that came from killing them. Now people understand how important wetlands are to people, plants, and animals. The United States government is now planning to return the Florida Everglades to its wild state.

The American alligator is one of the world's most successful stories of a species saved from extinction just in time. Thirty years ago there were only a few thousand wild alligators left in

the United States. Now there are more than two million.

But its relative in China is one of the most endangered animals on earth. Can you think of ways to save the Chinese alligator, too?

## Alligator Activity

Alligator holes give many animals easier access to water during the dry season when there is very little rain. See how this works by making your own gator hole. Here's what you'll need:

2 large bowls             1 cup water
1 measuring cup        1 cup soil

Ask an adult to help you gather your supplies, then fill each of the bowls with ½ cup soil and ½ cup water. Pat down the soil with your hands in one bowl so the mixture has an even surface. In the other bowl, dig a hole in the middle of the mixture. Watch what happens in the two bowls as the water evaporates. Do you see why other animals are dependent on the alligator hole for water?

## Gator Facts

- Baby alligators are called hatchlings. Hatchlings are approximately 6 to 8 inches at birth.
- The average alligator lives 35 to 50 years. Some gators have lived as long as 80 years.
- The average size of a female American alligator is 8.2 feet and the average size of a male is 11.2 feet.
- On dry land, an alligator can run at speeds of up to 20 miles per hour, but only for a very short time.
- In 1987, alligators were named the state reptile of Florida.
- Feeding alligators is illegal in the state of Florida. If fed, gators can associate humans with food and lose their natural fear of people.
- Learn more about the Florida Everglades at www.nps.gov/ever/.
- Chinese alligators are smaller than the American alligator. The Chinese alligator grows to a length of only 6 feet.
- The Chinese alligator lives only in the Yangtze River basin of China.